THE
WILD HORSES

BY
CARL R. GREEN
WILLIAM R. SANFORD

EDITED BY
DR. HOWARD SCHROEDER

Professor in Reading and Language Arts
Dept. of Elementary Education
Mankato State University

PRODUCED AND DESIGNED BY
BAKER STREET PRODUCTIONS
Mankato, MN

CRESTWOOD HOUSE
Mankato, Minnesota

LIBRARY OF CONGRESS CATALOGING IN PUBLICATION DATA
Sanford, William R. (William Reynolds).
  The wild horse.

  (Wildlife, habits & habitats)
  SUMMARY: Discusses the history, characteristics, habits, and future of
North America's wild horses.
    1. Wild horses—United States—Juvenile literature. 2. Mammals—United
States—Juvenile literature. (1. Wild horses. 2. Horses) I. Green, Carl R. II.
Title. III. Series.
SF360.3.U6S26   1985   599.72'5   85-13276
ISBN 0-89686-291-7 (lib. bdg.)

International Standard	Library of Congress
Book Number:	Catalog Card Number:
Library Binding 0-89686-291-7	85-13276

CRESTWOOD HOUSE
Hwy. 66 South, Box 3427
Mankato, MN 56002-3427

TABLE OF CONTENTS

INTRODUCTION:

"When will we see the wild horses?" Mike asked in an excited voice. He and Jennifer scanned the wide, flat beach of Assateague Island. The cool breeze off the Atlantic Ocean cooled their sweaty faces. The coastline of Virginia lay far behind them.

Dr. Perry smiled at his nephew and niece. He was panting after the three-mile bike ride. "We're in the National Wildlife Refuge now," Dr. Perry said. "About three hundred horses live on the island. We should see some soon."

"How did wild horses get to this island?" Jennifer asked.

"The horses have been here for hundreds of years," Dr. Perry told her. "Some people think they swam ashore from a wrecked Spanish ship. Others say that English settlers left them. However it happened, the horses returned to the wild."

Mike and Jennifer ran ahead of their uncle. Mike kept his camera ready. But where were the horses?

Suddenly, they heard the drumming of hoofs on the sand. A small band of pony-sized horses came galloping along the beach. A brown mare led the way, followed by four more mares and several foals. A large

Wild horses have been on Assateague Island for hundreds of years.

black stallion kept watch at the rear of the band, his head high and alert.

Mike forgot his camera. He stared at the graceful horses. Their long manes and tails flowed behind them as they ran.

''They're beautiful! But they're so small,'' Jennifer said.

Dr. Perry held her back. ''They look friendly, but they're truly wild. That stallion won't let you get too

Their long manes and tails are beautiful to see.

close," he warned. "And yes, as horses go, they are small. Most weigh less than seven hundred pounds (318 kg). They have to live on the island's small crop of grass and marsh plants."

The horses turned and ran into the surf. Several horses rolled over and splashed in the water. The foals pranced on the sand, like kids let out of school for the summer.

The stallion kept his eye on the visitors. He neighed loudly, and led the band into the shelter of some trees.

"I feel the wind picking up," Dr. Perry said. "We'll have to leave now. The island's highest point is only forty-seven feet (14.3 m) above sea level. In a bad storm, the horses have a hard time of it."

Mike quickly took a picture. "I wish I could take one of the horses home with me," he said.

"Come back in July," his uncle told him. "That's when the local fire fighters drive some of the horses over to Chincoteague Island. They sell the foals to raise money. The sales also keep the number of horses from getting out of control."

Mike and Jennifer looked at each other. They shook their heads sadly.

"We can't keep a horse in the city," Jennifer said. "Besides, they belong here. But we'll never forget the wild horses of Assateague."

CHAPTER ONE:

The world's first horses developed in North America thousands of years ago. The early horses were no bigger than a small fox. Scientists call them *Eohippus* (Greek for "dawn horse"). The tiny dawn horse had toes instead of hoofs.

Over thousands of years, *Eohippus* grew larger and more horse-like. The toes fused together to make a hoof. Known as *Equus*, these animals looked much like the modern horse. *Equus* herds crossed from North America into Asia at a time when Alaska and Siberia were joined by a land bridge. This migration took herds of wild horses into Asia, Europe, and Africa.

The horse died out in North America about the same time. Some people blame disease or over-hunting by Indians for their loss. No one knows exactly why *Equus* disappeared, however.

Horses return to the Americas

In the Old World, people tamed *Equus* and put them to work. Careful breeding created modern horses, now known as *Equus caballus*. Other members of the horse family include zebras, donkeys, and wild asses. But only the beautiful and useful *Equus caballus* gained a lasting spot in the hearts of kings and common people alike.

Spanish explorers brought horses back to North America in the early 1500's. The earliest Spanish explorers rode horseback through Mexico, Florida and the Southwest. But none of these horses were the ancestors of today's wild horses.

Ancestors of today's wild horses were brought to North America by early Spanish explorers.

In 1598, Juan de Õnate set out to explore the Rio Grande valley in present-day New Mexico. Õnate ran into warlike Apache Indians, who stole many of his horses. The Indians ate some of the animals, but they also learned to ride them. By 1659, the Spanish in Santa Fe were fighting off raids by hard-riding Apaches.

In 1680, the Pueblo Indians went to war against the Spanish and captured many more horses. The fast new method of transportation spread like wildfire. Fifty years later, tribes that lived as far east as Ohio and as far north as western Canada, were using horses.

The American Indian soon found ways to use the horse.

Indians take to a new way of life

The horse changed the western Indian's way of life. When they learned to ride horses, most tribes gave up farming. The Indians became expert riders. They rode great distances to find game. A good horseman was greatly admired, and taming a wild horse was seen as a test of courage. In some tribes, young Indians had to steal a horse from another tribe before they could become warriors.

The Indians also used horses as work animals. When they moved their camps, the Plains Indians packed their goods in bundles tied between two poles. When hitched to a horse, these travois, as they were called, made travel easier. During times of famine, the Indians also ate horse meat.

Wild horse herds grew rapidly

Many Indian horses escaped from their owners. These animals, often called mustangs, found the grasslands a perfect place to live. In a short time, large numbers of wild horses were roaming on the prairies.

11

The Indians worked out ways to take new mounts from the wild herds. In the "relay," groups of riders spread out over the plains. Each group took turns chasing a herd of mustangs until the horses were tired out. Then the Indians roped the horses they wanted. But that was only the first step. The Indians then had the hard job of training the wild horses for riding.

The age of the wild horse on the Great Plains lasted two hundred years (during the 1600's and 1700's). By the early 1800's, at least two million wild horses were running free in North America. Half of these horses were in Texas. The others were scattered over the rest of the Southwest. In time, wild horses also appeared in the Northwest. These herds were started by horses that escaped from white settlers. Wild horse herds did not spread east of the Mississippi, however. The eastern woodlands did not provide enough good grazing.

Settlers declare war

The coming of barbed wire ended the days of the wild horse in many parts of the West. The fences cut the mustang herds off from their grazing lands. Farmers and ranchers shot mustangs on sight. They said the wild horses ate grass needed for cattle and sheep. In addition,

Farmers and ranchers tried to get rid of wild horses in the late 1800's.

valuable domestic horses sometimes ran off to join the wild herds.

Cowboys, known as "mustangers," joined in the war against the wild horses. The mustangers caught and tamed the horses in order to sell them. They sold large numbers of mustangs at prices that averaged about ten dollars a head. By comparison, a horse was worth ten times as much in the East. Another market opened up for the mustangers in the 1890's. The British bought thousands of horses to ship to South Africa for use in the Boer War.

Governments join the attack

As long as a need for horses existed, cowboys kept on rounding up the mustangs. But the automobile changed that. No one was interested in taming wild horses when the price fell to rock bottom in the years before World War I. Left alone, the size of the wild herds increased rapidly. In 1925, the United States was home to over a million wild horses.

Government officials in some western states worried that the herds were becoming too large. They allowed roundups of wild horses for sale as pet food. Laws were passed that allowed people to kill unbranded, owner-less horses. By then, a wild horse was worth only two or three dollars at a pet food plant.

In 1934, Congress voted to limit the number of animals allowed to graze on public lands. Wild horses were seen as pests that overgrazed the grasslands. The horses were shot whenever they were found in protected areas. By the end of the 1950's, more than 100,000 of Nevada's wild horses had been rounded up. Most were killed and made into feed for chickens.

Without laws to protect them, wild horses seemed doomed to extinction. No one seemed to care about these small, dusty relatives of the domestic horse.

CHAPTER TWO:

Look closely at the next saddle horse you see. It's an animal that hasn't changed much since horses were first tamed thousands of years ago. Imagine a wild horse standing next to the saddle horse. The wild horse will be nearly a carbon copy.

The two horses look alike because all North American wild horses are descended from domestic horses. Scientists, in fact, prefer to call them feral horses. A feral animal is any domestic animal that has returned to life in the wild.

A "feral horse" is a domestic horse that has gone back to being wild.

Once domestic horses run away, they adapt quickly to their new life. They have keen senses, and their speed makes it easy for them to escape from their enemies. When their foals are born, they grow up as wild as any other free-roaming horse.

Vital statistics

Experts divide wild horses into four groups by age and sex. From birth to one year, males and females are both known as foals. During its second year, a male foal is called a colt; a female foal is called a filly. As the colt matures, he becomes a young stud, or a bachelor male. The filly grows up to become a mare. A bachelor male that has captured his own band of mares is called a stallion. A typical band is made up of one stallion plus a number of mares, young studs, colts, fillies, and foals. When several bands share a range, the larger group is known as a herd.

Mustangers once loved to tell tall tales of giant wild stallions that ran like the wind. Wild horses do run fast, but they are almost never giants. A typical wild stallion seldom stands taller then fifteen hands. (A hand is four inches, or 10.2 cm. Height is measured from the front hoof to the top of the horse's back.) The smaller mares measure about thirteen hands high. Any horse that measures less than thirteen hands is referred to as a pony. By comparison, a modern race horse averages sixteen hands high.

Wild horses are small only when compared to other horses. Wild stallions weigh up to one thousand pounds (450 kg). Mares average about eight hundred pounds (360 kg). The food supply greatly affects the weight of the horses. In areas where grass, salt, and water are scarce, fully-grown wild horses may weigh as little as 650 pounds (295 kg).

About one-half of all wild horses are reddish-brown, a color known as bay. Other common colors are grey, black, white, and dun (a greyish-brown). Spotted and pinto horses can also be found in many wild horse herds. Most horses have black manes and tails, but brown, grey, and white manes are also common.

This beautiful black stallion was photographed in Wyoming.

A horse is as old as its teeth

Starvation, disease, and accidents kill many wild horses. Old age for a wild horse is twelve to fourteen years, compared to a domestic horse's life span of fifteen to twenty years. Experts can tell the age of a horse by the number and condition of its teeth. A stallion has forty teeth, a mare has thirty-six. Colts and fillies have only twenty-four.

Wild horses feed mostly on desert grasses. Their front teeth nip off the grass, and the molars chew it up. In time, sand and tough grasses grind down the horse's teeth. If the teeth wear down to the gums, the animal will likely starve.

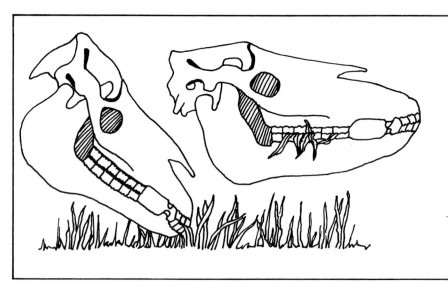

The horse's front teeth nip off grass, and the back molars chew it up.

Four gaits using the middle toe

Scientists tell us that horses walk and run on their middle toenails! Over the years, the middle toe of early horses became larger and the other toes were lost. Today, that huge, hard "toenail" is called a hoof. With its long legs and hard hoofs the horse is one of the fastest runners around. Wild horses have been clocked at thirty-five miles per hour (56 kph).

Wild horses have four natural gaits, or ways of moving. The gaits are the walk, trot, pace, and gallop. A walking horse moves its feet one at a time: left front, right rear, right front, left rear. In this way, the horse is always supported by two or three of its legs. To move faster, the horse breaks into a trot. The trot moves two feet at the same time: left front and right rear, then right front and left rear.

A pacing horse moves at about the same speed as a trotting horse. In this gait, the two feet on the left move at the same time, followed by the two right feet. For high speed, however, the horse changes into a gallop. A galloping horse springs forward off its left rear foot. The right rear and the left front feet strike next, followed by the right front foot. In slow motion, you will hear a four-beat rhythm as the hoofs strike one after the other. By pivoting on its front foot, a galloping horse can turn quickly to the side.

A keen brain and sharp senses

Horses are smart animals. Some experts put their brain in sixth place among the animals. On this list, they're right behind the apes, whales and dolphins, the elephant, and the dog.

Wild horses show different personalities. They can be friendly or fierce, hot-tempered or calm. Only rarely do wild horses attack people or other animals. Most attacks come when a stallion feels that his band of horses is in danger.

Wild horses see the world differently than humans. Along with being color blind, they tend not to "see" objects that don't move. If the wind is blowing toward you, you can sit quietly near a band of grazing horses and never be seen. With eyes set on the sides of their heads, horses have a wide field of vision. A small movement of his head allows a grazing stallion to watch for danger from all sides. This is a useful ability, because wild horses are good at seeing the slightest movement, both far and near. Since their judgement of distance is poor, however, they avoid jumping.

The wild horse's keen senses of smell and hearing make up for any lack of vision. When sniffing the air, the horse widens its nostrils to help pick up more scent. They can smell an enemy coming long before they can see it. They also can find hidden water holes entirely

Wild horses can smell an enemy long before they see them.

by scent. Similarly, a watchful stallion can hear sounds too faint for human ears. But a stallion doesn't need to "hear" the footsteps of an enemy. Each step sets off tiny vibrations which wild horses can pick up through their hoofs.

Sensitive skins

Horses have a higher body temperature than humans (about two degrees Fahrenheit higher). During hot weather, they overheat easily, so they sweat to keep their skin cool. A hard run will leave wild horses streaked with foamy sweat. To cool down, they shiver and twitch their skin. Twitching, along with switching the tail, also gets rid of insects.

A wild horse's skin is sensitive to the touch. The horses often rub against trees or rocks to scratch themselves. They also roll on their backs in sand or mud. They do this "wallowing" with all four legs sticking up in the air.

Wild horses need all of these abilities. Domestic horses can depend on their owners for food and shelter. The wild horse herds, however, must adapt to the harsh habitat in which they live.

The wild horse must adapt to areas that often do not have much grass.

Winters can be harsh in areas where wild horses live. These horses live in the Badlands of South Dakota.

CHAPTER THREE:

Wild horses roam across a lonely, barren land. They live in the shadow of high mountains, and on scrub desert plains. Their habitat often seems to be mostly rocks and sand.

Only twelve states have wild horse populations. The largest herds can be found in the back country of Nevada, Wyoming, Oregon, New Mexico, and California. A few herds live in Utah, Idaho, Colorado, Montana, and Arizona. On the east coast, the Assateague Island herd wanders freely across the border that divides the island between Maryland and Virginia.

Food is in short supply

The barren habitat left to most wild horses doesn't grow good grass. As a result, wild horses spend about half their daylight hours feeding. Each horse needs over twenty pounds (9 kg) of plant food a day. When the grass is gone, they eat almost anything that grows. One naturalist in Wyoming counted twenty-eight different plants in their diet. These include purple moor grass, small flowering plants, saltbrush, greasewood, and sagebrush. They also nibble on tree bark.

With food in short supply, wild horses keep moving. They drift slowly from one bunch of dry grass to the next. Each band stays within its own home range, unless driven out by a lack of water and food. In bad times, the horses sometimes eat their own droppings for whatever food value is left. Once in a while, a hungry horse eats a poisonous plant, such as locoweed, and dies.

Wild horses also need water and salt. In hot weather, they drink twice a day from water holes and streams. Because other animals also use the water holes, the stallion often leads the way, checking for danger. At his signal, the rest of the band runs forward to drink. On a warm day, the horses will wade into the water up to their bellies. Most habitats also have a salt lick that the horses visit. There they find special rocks which contain salt.

Stallions rule their bands

In the old days, wild horse habitats supported herds that numbered in the thousands. Within those big herds, stallions kept their own bands of mares and foals intact. Today, the big herds are almost gone. Most wild horses live in small bands.

When a stallion matures, he gathers a band of two to twenty mares under his rule. In most cases, he will have to fight other males for each mare. A typical band has about eight mares. Once a mare joins his band, the stallion will defend her to the death.

The stallion keeps a watchful guard. Should a bear, mountain lion, or human being come too close, he will sound a warning cry. The band gets ready to run at his next command. A young stud who comes too close, however, will be met by a sudden, violent attack. When stallions grow old, they often lose their mares to younger, stronger males. When that happens, the old stallion wanders off to live by himself.

Mares give birth to equal numbers of male and female foals. A stallion with nine mares, therefore, must be on guard against at least eight bachelor males. A stallion who cannot protect his mares will soon lose them. Like a good shepherd, a stallion keeps his band close together.

Some stallions are more powerful than others. These "kings" can claim the best grazing areas for their mares. All stallions mark out a line between their own territory and that of other bands. If a strange band moves in, the stallion puts on a fierce display of flashing hoofs and teeth. In most cases, the intruders leave without a fight.

Wild horses sometimes stay together for protection.

Stallions sometimes join their bands into a herd. In times past, when wolves hunted in large packs, a herd was the best way to protect the foals. The stallions formed a ring around the herd. That left them ready to lash out with their sharp hoofs at any wolf who came too close. Herds also form when the wild horse population fills up its habitat.

Young studs compete for mares

A second type of band exists in wild horse habitats. Male horses that can't attract mares of their own roam in bachelor bands. These bands contain three- to eight-year-old males. These young studs are full of energy, but aren't ready to take on the more powerful stallions. The studs stage play-fights with each other to sharpen their fighting skills.

Once in a while, several young studs will work together to raid a stallion's mares. One stud snorts loudly to catch the stallion's attention. When the stallion rushes to drive the stranger away, the other studs try

Young studs form bachelor bands.

to cut a mare out of the band. This is clever, but usually doesn't work. The stallion turns and chases off the younger horses.

Mares have their own leader

Within the band, one older mare serves as a leader. The stallion rules the band, but the lead mare picks the route the band will follow. She also passes the stallion's signals on to the others. The lead mare and her foal get to drink first at water holes. The stallion treats her as his ''favorite,'' and the other mares seek out her company. If a young stallion pushes her too hard, the lead mare may turn around and bite him!

Mares seldom fight with each other. A mare will sometimes "steal" the foal of another mare in the band, however. If successful, the kidnapper lets the new foal nurse next to her own foal. Most of the time, mares don't like strange foals. If one comes too close, they will kick at the foal to drive it away.

Mares belong to the stallion who rounds them up. Once a stallion selects a mare, she stays with him. An all-mare band can develop, however, when a stallion is killed. The band remains on its own until a new stallion claims the mares.

Horses affect the habitat

A wild horse band has a lasting affect on its habitat. Deer and antelope graze nearby, trusting that the stallion will alert them to danger. In winter, smaller animals benefit when the horses break the ice at the water holes. Grazing horses also pass seeds through their bodies when they eat. Thus, their droppings reseed the land for future grazing.

Naturalists are still trying to learn more about the wild horse. It's not easy to get close to them. But careful studies have given us a fairly good picture of their life cycle.

CHAPTER FOUR:

Wild horses live at peace with their habitat and with the cycle of the seasons. Their lives follow a cycle that began with the ancient horse known as *Equus*.

Spring brings new foals

Wild horse trails are easy to follow in the spring. Over the year, the hard hoofs of the band have packed down the soil. This hard ground holds water, and the horses' droppings add a rich fertilizer. Green ribbons of grass appear along the trails as if by magic.

In late May, a band of wild horses moved out of the Nevada valley where it had spent the winter. The lead mare led the way upward into the high canyons. The horses nibbled at the new grass as they walked along the trail.

A hungry mountain lion watched as the band entered a mountain meadow. The big white stallion caught its scent, and snorted loudly. The band heard the danger signal and broke into a gallop. The lion gave up and went hunting for easier prey.

The mares were heavy with the foals they had carried for eleven months. On this day, the horses galloped on to a water hole and plunged into its welcome coolness. In a few minutes they drank about ten gallons (38 liters) of water. Then they moved into the shade of some small trees to rest and graze.

A three-year-old bay mare rolled over on her side in the grass. It was time for her first foal to be born. A half hour later, the male foal lay beside her, his eyes already open. He struggled to stand up. The thin legs

A new foal seems to be all legs.

seemed barely strong enough to hold the small body. Finally, the foal stood on shaky legs. The mare whinnied softly. The foal found one of the mare's teats and began sucking the rich milk.

Two hours later, the foal was trotting beside the mare. He followed her while she grazed, flicking his tail at a swarm of pesky flies. The stallion came by to sniff at this new foal. After a moment, he wheeled away to round up the other mares. The lead mare led the way upward to a meadow filled with new grass and wildflowers. Within the month, four other foals were born to the band.

Summer is a time for mating

In July the temperature rose to over a hundred degrees Fahrenheit (40 degrees C). The band of horses was making its daily trip to the water hole. Their hoofs sent up clouds of dust from the sandy valley floor. The last rain had fallen weeks ago. The desert grass was turning brown. The water hole was also drying up. If it disappeared, the band would have to leave its home range to find the water it needed.

The band's five foals included two colts and three fillies. Toward evening the heat broke, and the foals became playful. They ran around, making sudden starts and stops. A black foal kicked up his heels and tossed his head, just like the white stallion sometimes did. A spotted filly nosed around in the bushes. The whirr of a rattlesnake ready to strike sent the curious filly hurrying back to safety.

For the older horses, it was the mating season. The stallion was kept busy chasing off eager young studs. But one black stud was not frightened off by the stallion's squeals of rage. The two strong males faced each other and reared up on their back legs. They slashed at each other with their front hoofs. Dust boiled up around the fighters. The white stallion bit the black horse on the neck, drawing blood. Beaten, the black stud backed away. The white stallion was still "king."

In the days that followed, the stallion mated with each mare. Mares are ready to bear foals when they are two or three years old. In a given year, up to ninety percent of the mares will carry a foal. The stallion drove his

Most mares will have a foal every year.

own two-year-old fillies out of the band rather than mate with them. The fillies were soon added to another stallion's band. Naturalists say that this instinctive behavior keeps the stallions from mating with their own offspring. If they did, the foals might be born deformed.

Fall is a social time

The fall days brought cooler weather. The band of horses had moved only about twenty miles (32 km) from where the first foal was born. Good grass was getting hard to find. The hungry horses ate brush, weeds, and tree bark.

The colts often played and fought with each other. The play-fights were training for the day they would become stallions. The colts reared and pawed at each other, teeth snapping. The combat usually ended with the colts rubbing noses with each other.

Mutual grooming was another common activity. The grooming was usually done by a mare and her foal, two foals, or two mares of equal rank. When the stallion groomed, it was with the lead mare. The grooming horses nibbled at itchy spots on each other's neck, mane, legs, and tail. Naturalists think that the grooming strengthens friendship bonds within the band.

The band spent the night in the shelter of some small trees. The white stallion never fully relaxed. He stood on three legs, his left hind leg bent and barely touching the ground. In this position he dozed lightly, ready for danger. Some of the mares lay down and tucked their legs beneath them. The foals slept on their sides, safe under the watchful guard of the stallion.

Winter tests the band

The weather changed during November. The first snow fell in the Nevada canyon. The temperature dropped sharply, but the wild horses didn't seem to feel the cold. They turned their backs to the wind and waited for the storm to blow itself out.

An unusual event upset the band of horses one morning. A naturalist tried to sneak in close to take some pictures. The stallion caught her scent on the breeze. He trotted toward her, then stopped. His muscles rippled as he snorted and danced in place. The naturalist was frightened. She stood very still.

The stallion finally turned and herded his band toward a nearby ridge. One young filly stopped to graze. She got a nip on her hind leg for disobeying orders. When the band reached the ridge, the stallion snorted loudly and rose up on his hind legs. His loud battle cry filled

A stallion will often herd his band away from danger.

the air. Then the band galloped down the back side of the ridge.

Safe once more, the band stopped to feed. The horses chopped at the snow with their front hoofs to find the half-frozen grass. They also nibbled at a holly tree. The snow hid a crop of acorns under a wild oak tree. This was lucky, for wild horses will stuff themselves with acorns—and too many acorns will poison a horse.

Back in the canyon, the naturalist thought about what she had seen. She knew that cold weather was only one of the dangers faced by wild horses. One young stud had been limping, perhaps from a pulled muscle. She guessed that he had stepped into a hole made by a small animal. If the leg had been broken, the stud would probably have died.

The days when grizzly bears and wolves preyed on the wild horses were over. These predators no longer roam the wild horse ranges. Today, coyotes will sometimes pull down a stray foal. The most dangerous animal predator is the mountain lion. After these big cats taste horse meat, it becomes their favorite food.

The naturalist hiked back to her camp. The stallion and his band seemed safe for the moment. She hoped that their future would be equally secure.

This stallion is alert to danger!

CHAPTER FIVE:

Until recent years, wild horses were thought to be a pest. No laws protected them, and thousands were killed every year. Only a few horse lovers worried that these beautiful animals were marked for extinction.

Protection under the law

The first federal law protecting wild horses was passed in 1959. The law is often called the Wild Horse Annie Bill, in honor of Mrs. Velma Johnston. ''Wild Horse Annie'' Johnston took the case for the wild horses to the public. She let people know that the horses were being hunted from airplanes. The low-flying airplanes drove the bands out of their hidden canyons. Once they were out on the open plains, the horses were easily killed.

The Wild Horse Annie Bill outlawed the hunting of wild horses from airplanes or motor vehicles. The law did not stop the killing, however. Ranchers still blamed the wild horses for ruining grazing lands and for stealing their tame mares. The National Mustang Association tried to have the wild horses listed as an endangered species, but without success.

Wild Horse Annie did not give up. She kept on telling people about the killing of the wild horses. Thousands of school children wrote to Congress, asking for better laws. Finally, Public Law 92-195 was passed in 1971. Known as the Wild Free-Roaming Horse and Burro Act, the law gave federal protection to the remaining wild horses. No one is allowed to capture, brand, or kill a wild horse or burro.

New problems develop

In 1971, fewer than ten thousand wild horses were left alive. But wild horse populations grow rapidly. Ten years later, there were about 55,000 horses roaming the western states. The increase meant that the horses wouldn't become extinct. But the rapid growth created new problems.

Wild horses live in areas where cattle can't find enough food. Too many horses grazing on this desert land quickly ruin the grass. Federal laws, however, make it hard to control the population growth. Land management workers have had to find new ways to deal with the horses.

One method is to count the number of wild horses in a region. If too many horses are living there, the excess animals are rounded up. The workers then put these horses up for adoption! The Adopt-a-Horse program gives the horses to anyone who will take proper care of them. Some horses have even been sent to Mexico to be trained as cow ponies and show horses. These controls have brought the numbers down to around 45,000.

Are wild horses a pest?

Naturalists and ranchers still argue over the effect of the wild horses on their habitat. The naturalists say that the horses do not seriously damage the environment. They point out that the horses spread grass seeds and fertilize the soil. In addition, they break trails

Helicopters are often used to round up wild horses.

through the snow that other animals can use.

The ranchers also have a strong argument. Roaming wild horse bands cross highways and cause danger to passing cars. The horses kill the grass by overgrazing. They break down fences, trample crops, and dirty water holes. Many ranchers have also lost prize mares to raids by wild stallions.

The argument has been solved for the moment by setting aside refuges for the wild horses. In the East, you can see wild horses on Assateague Island, off the Maryland-Virginia coast. In the West, two typical refuges are Pryor Mountain Wild Horse Refuge in Montana and the Owyhee Desert in northern Nevada.

A trip into these remote areas is well worth the time and trouble. For many people, the wild horse is a symbol of natural beauty and freedom. You can stand on a Montana ridge and thrill to the sight of two stallions fighting for their mares. Or you can smile at the eager young colts as they play-fight.

The wild horses can be a problem, but they do remind us of our ties with nature. It's a part of us that too often gets lost in the cement canyons of our cities.

For many people, the wild horse is a symbol of freedom.

MAP:

Assateague
Island

The shaded areas
show where most
wild horses live
in the United States.

INDEX/GLOSSARY:

WILDLIFE
HABITS & HABITAT

READ AND ENJOY THE SERIES:

If you would like to know more about all kinds of wildlife, you should take a look at the other books in this series.

You'll find books on bald eagles and other birds. Books on alligators and other reptiles. There are books about deer and other big-game animals. And there are books about sharks and other creatures that live in the ocean.

In all of the books you will learn that life in the wild is not easy. But you will also learn what people can do to help wildlife survive. So read on!

DATE DUE

SEP 26	MAY 02		
OCT 27	MAY 13		
DEC 1			
DEC 4			
JAN 5			
JAN 5 FEB 12			
MAR 19 MAR 26			
APR 06			
APR 21 MAY 22			
MAY 22			
OCT 14			
OCT 28			
NOV 4			
FEB 08			